Your Food

Claire Llewellyn

W
FRANKLIN WATTS
LONDON • SYDNEY

This edition 2004

Franklin Watts
96 Leonard Street
London
EC2A 4XD

Franklin Watts Australia
45-51 Huntley Street
Alexandria
NSW 2015

Series editor: Sarah Peutrill
Art director: Jonathan Hair
Design: Kirstie Billingham
Illustrations: James Evans
Photographs: Ray Moller unless otherwise acknowledged
Picture research: Diana Morris
Series consultant: Lynn Huggins-Cooper

Acknowledgments:
Professor N. Russell/Science Photo Library: 18cr
Sinclair Stammers/Science Photo Library: 24t

With thanks to our models: Emilia, Holly, Jerome, Lewis, Mandalena and Wilf

A CIP record for this book is available from the British Library.

Dewey Classification 613.2

ISBN: 0 7496 5647 6

Printed in Hong Kong/China

Look After Yourself

Contents

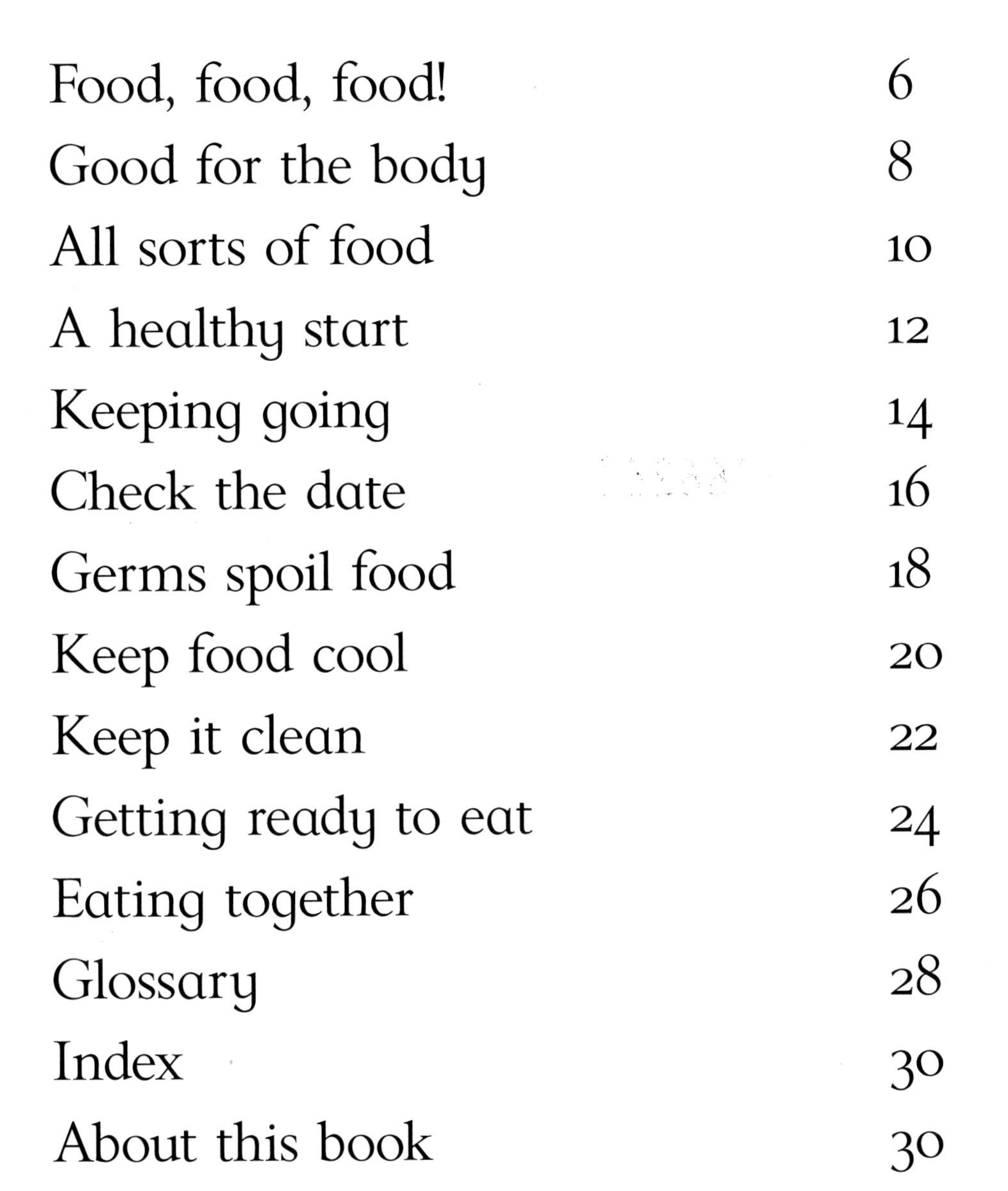

Food, food, food!

Food is important to all of us. It plays a big part in our lives. There are so many sorts of food. How do we know what to choose?

There is so much food to choose from. It can be hard to know what to eat.

We see food everywhere - not just in shops and cafés, but in cinemas, swimming pools and parks. Food is all around us. Why do we need it so much?

We are never far from food. It is sold in all sorts of places.

Good for the body

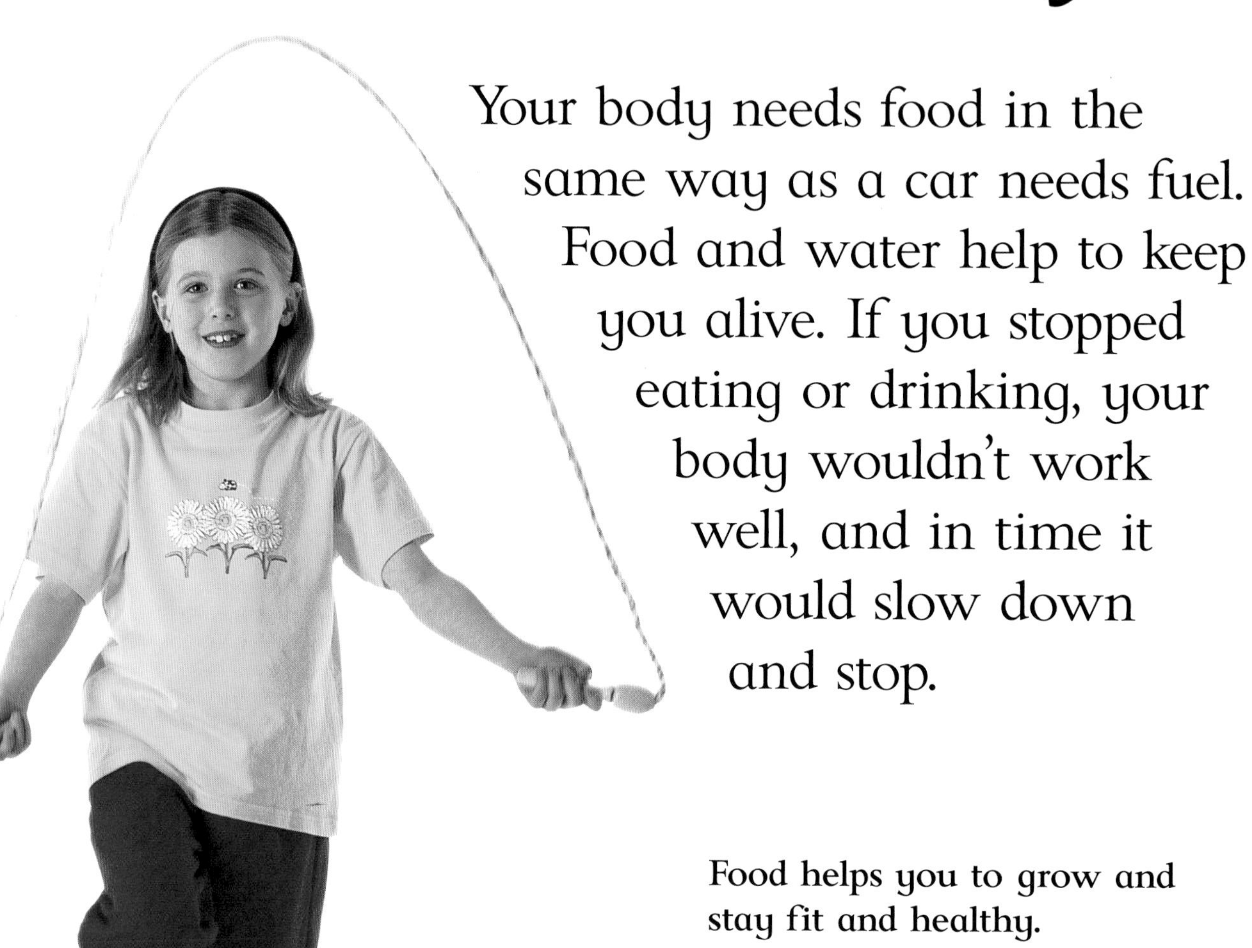

Your body needs food in the same way as a car needs fuel. Food and water help to keep you alive. If you stopped eating or drinking, your body wouldn't work well, and in time it would slow down and stop.

Food helps you to grow and stay fit and healthy.

We put foods into four groups. The foods in each group help us in different ways.

Pasta, potatoes, rice and bread give us energy.

All sorts of food

You probably have a food that you love to eat. It may be peanut butter, chicken curry, strawberries or ice cream. Enjoy your favourite food but eat other foods as well.

You need to eat more than just your favourite food!

If you eat only one type of food your body won't get everything it needs. You need to eat lots of different foods to stay healthy.

Are there any foods I shouldn't eat?

No food is bad for you, but try not to eat too many sugary foods. Sugar harms your teeth!

Most of us like sweet foods but they make our teeth decay.

A healthy start

When you wake in the morning,
your body needs food.
A good breakfast is very important.
It gives you the energy to start your day.

Here are some of the foods people eat at breakfast. What do you like to have?

During the day, you think, work and play. This uses every part of your body.

Breakfast helps you to be active. It helps you to get up and go.

Our bodies are busy all day long.

Don't skip your breakfast! You need it!

Keeping going

By the end of the morning, you begin to feel hungry. Your energy starts to run low. It's time to have some lunch. Eating something from each food group will keep you healthy.

My tummy is rumbling – it must be lunchtime.

This is a healthy lunch. What do you like to eat at lunchtime?

Everyone needs a snack sometimes between meals. Fruit, yogurts or cereal bars are a healthy choice and help us to keep going.

At the end of the day, we have one more meal. This gives us energy until bedtime and allows our bodies to work all night long.

Check the date

Some food comes in packets or tins. It lasts a very long time. A date on the packaging tells you when it should be thrown away.

Tinned tuna lasts for five years.

Dried pasta - two years

Tinned salmon - three years

Tea and coffee - two years

Sweetcorn - three years

These foods must be kept in the freezer.

Some food is frozen. If you keep it in a freezer it lasts for a month or more.

Other foods are fresh and last only a few days.

Bread rolls - two days

The 'Use-by' date tells you how long the food will last.

Cress - four days

Fish - one day

Germs spoil food

What are germs? I've never seen any.

Tiny things called germs spoil fresh food. You can't see them, but they are everywhere.

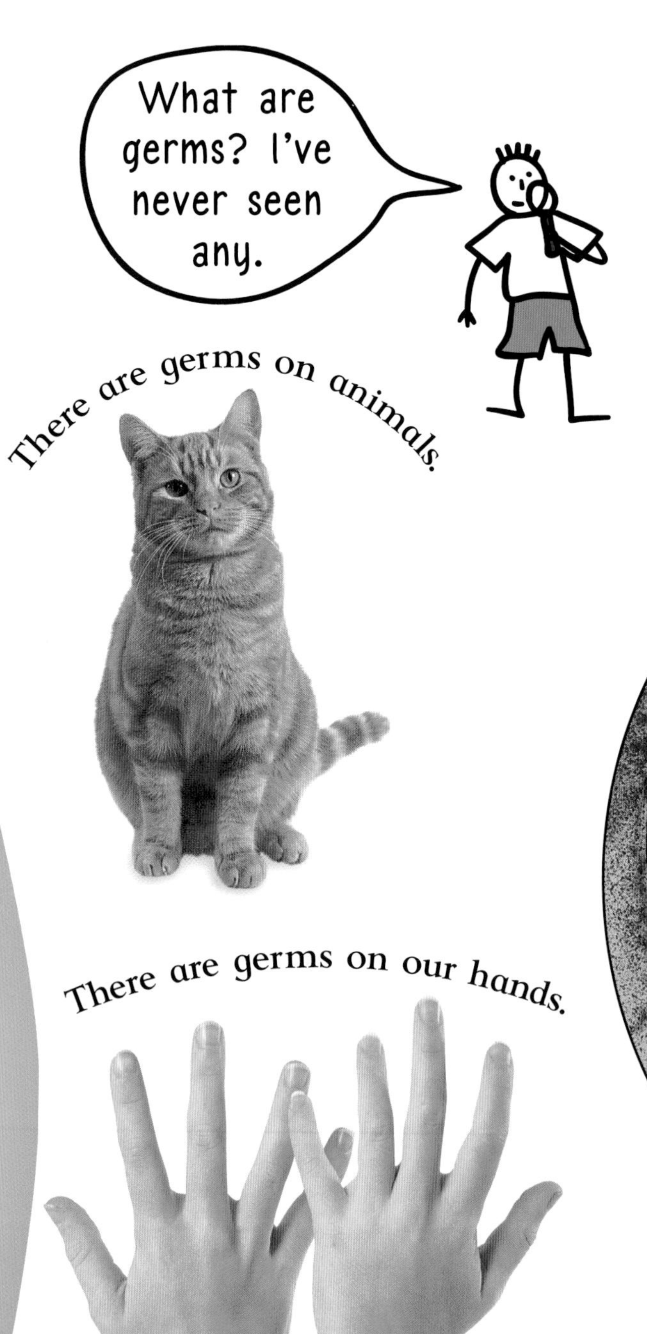

There are germs on animals.

There are germs on our hands.

There are germs in the air around us.

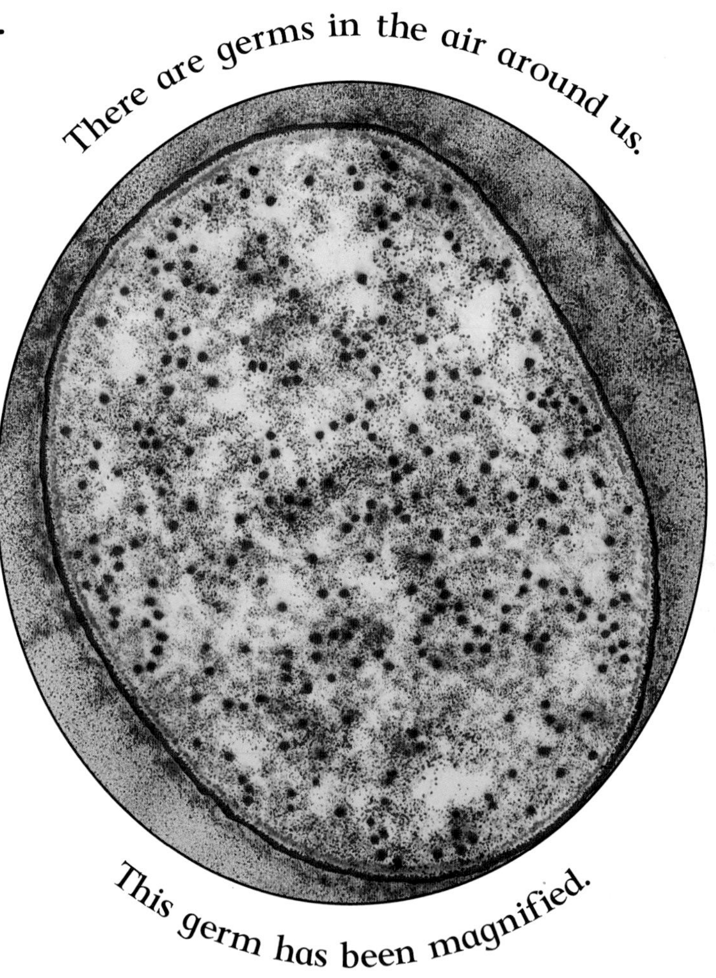

This germ has been magnified.

Germs like places that are warm or damp or dirty. In places like these, germs feed and grow. Then they begin to spread. They spoil fresh food and make it go bad.

Cheese goes mouldy if you keep it too long.

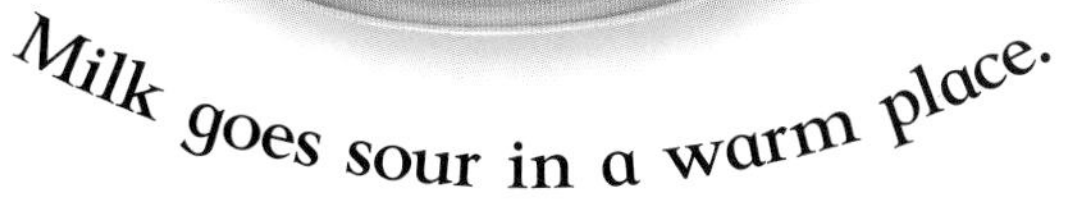

Milk goes sour in a warm place.

Old tomatoes start to rot.

Bad food tastes nasty and can make you really ill.

Keep food cool

Fresh foods such as meat and fish need to be put in the fridge. This helps to stop germs spoiling them. The cold helps to keep food fresh.

These are some of the foods that we store in the fridge. What else do you put in your fridge?

Fresh foods last longer in the fridge, but in time they start to go bad. The fridge will not keep them fresh for ever. Remember to check the 'use-by' date on food before you eat it.

When food has passed its 'use-by' date throw it in the bin.

Keep it clean

Before you touch food, make sure everything is clean. Always wash your hands with soap and water. This helps to get rid of germs.

It is important to wash your hands before cooking or eating. Do you always remember?

Wipe the table and worktops before you start. Make sure all the kitchen tools are clean.

Germs love dirty cloths. Make sure yours is clean.

Always wash fresh vegetables, fruit and salad. This helps to get rid of germs from the soil.

Remember, you can't always see the dirt on things.

Getting ready to eat

Always cover fresh food and keep it in the fridge until you are ready to eat it. If you don't, flies may land on it. They spread germs that can make you ill.

Flies land on all sorts of muck. They spread germs onto your food.

Keep fresh food in the fridge until you are ready to eat it.

Cats and dogs carry germs, too. Don't allow animals to come too near the table. Don't let them touch your food.

Pets carry all sorts of germs. Keep them away from food.

Eating together

It's good to share food with family or friends. Make sure everything you use is clean.

Bring the food out when you're ready to eat it.

Put food away at the end of a meal and leave the kitchen clean.

At the end of the meal, it's time to clear up. Throw away old food. Cover good food and put it back in the fridge. Then wash all the dishes and leave everything clean ... so that it is ready for next time.

Glossary

active to be moving, working and doing things

energy the power we get from food, which makes us able to work and grow, and keep warm

fats something found in foods, such as cheese and butter, that gives us energy

fresh fresh food has been made or picked recently. It is not stale, dried, tinned or frozen

frozen when something is so cold it turns hard. Frozen food can be stored for a long time

fuel something, such as petrol or wood, that gives energy when it is burned

germs tiny living things that can spread disease and make you feel ill. Germs are too small to see

harm to hurt

healthy	fit and well
magnified	made to look bigger
mouldy	Mould is a green or black fungus that sometimes grows on food and spoils it
packaging	the paper, plastic or metal container in which food is often wrapped
pulses	dried seeds, such as peas, beans and lentils
sour	having a sharp, nasty taste
to spoil	to go bad
sugar	something that is found in many foods and makes them taste sweet
tooth decay	when teeth go bad and have holes in them
use-by date	the date on packaging that tells you how long food is safe to eat

Index

About this book

Learning the principles of how to keep healthy and clean is one of life's most important skills. **Look After Yourself** is a series aimed at young children who are just beginning to develop these skills. **Your Food** looks at how to have a healthy diet and teaches simple food safety rules. To encourage a positive relationship with food it does not dwell on so-called 'unhealthy' foods, but stresses a balanced diet. For older children the book could be used as a starting point to explore other food safety issues, for example using equipment such as knives correctly and cooking food.

Here are a few suggestions for activities children could try:

Pages 6-7 Discuss the range of places where food can be bought - supermarkets, local food stores, outdoor markets etc.

Pages 8-9 If appropriate, introduce the correct terms for the four food groups - carbohydrates, proteins, vitamins and minerals, and fats. Children could write food diaries for a week and work out to which group each food belongs. They could then decide whether they have had a balanced diet.

Pages 10-11 Do a class or group survey of favourite foods and present the results in a bar chart.

Pages 12-13 Investigate what people eat for breakfast in different parts of the world by writing to pen-friends or relatives abroad.

Pages 14-15 Discuss favourite snack foods. Which ones help children to 'keep going' longer?

Pages 16-17 Collect together packaging from various different types of food and then try to find the use-by dates.

Pages 18-19 Write 'a day in the life of a germ' story. The germ may be living on a dog, then get transferred to a hand when someone strokes the dog, and so on.

Pages 20-21 Draw stick people and decide what they might say about keeping food in the fridge.

Pages 22-27 Make a fruit salad, following the same procedure as the two children here: keeping everything clean, washing the fruit and keeping the food in the fridge until it's time to eat.

Bye!